Ancient Egypt
in Lace and Color

Ancient Egypt
in Lace and Color

Anna Dalvi

Cooperative Press
Cleveland, OH

Library of Congress Control Number: 2012945222
ISBN 13: 978-1-937513-12-2
First Edition
Published by Cooperative Press
http://www.cooperativepress.com

Patterns, charts, and text © 2012, Anna Dalvi
Photos © 2012, Caro Sheridan
Additional photography by
Nick Murway and Shannon Okey

Model: Arabella Proffer

Every effort has been made to ensure that all the information in this book is accurate at the time of publication, however Cooperative Press neither endorses nor guarantees the content of external links referenced in this book.

If you have questions or comments about this book, or need information about licensing, custom editions, special sales, or academic/corporate purchases, please contact Cooperative Press: info@cooperativepress.com or 13000 Athens Ave C288, Lakewood, OH 44107 USA

SPECIAL THANKS
RAH Egypt Flora and RAH Egypt Web Set fonts by Robyn A. Harton, available at myfonts.com

FOR COOPERATIVE PRESS

Senior Editor: Shannon Okey
Technical Editor: Kate Atherley
Assistant Editor: Elizabeth Green Musselman

To Aneesh
And to Linnéa, Axel, and Viggo
Thanks for always cheering me on.

TABLE OF CONTENTS

INTRODUCTION

In ancient Egypt, color was a very important part of the arts and life. *Iwen*, the ancient Egyptian name for color, could also mean appearance, character, being, or nature. So the use of color in arts and myths had great symbolic significance. An object's or person's color would give a clue to its nature.

Six colors were used in the Egyptian art of the Old Kingdom (third millennium BCE): green, red, white, black, yellow, and blue.

Green (Wadj)

Green was the color of new vegetation and new life. The hieroglyph used for Wadj was the same hieroglyph used for the papyrus plant, and also for malachite.

The Fields of Malachite were the land of the blessed dead. And contrary to the emotions that we tend to associate with death, the place was meant to bring happy feelings. Green malachite was a symbol of joy. To do "green things" was to do beneficial and life-affirming things. Perhaps a little like the green movement today.

Osiris, the king of the dead, was often depicted with green skin. The Eye of Horus amulet was usually made out of green stone. It was a healing and protective amulet.

Red (Desher)

Red was the symbol of anger and fire, chaos, and rage. It was also the color of the desert, which the ancient Egyptians called *deshret*. Deshret was the opposite of Kemet, the fertile black land along the Nile.

Seth, the god of the desert, storms and chaos, had red eyes and red hair.

White (Hedj)

White was the color of sacredness, simplicity, and purity. In many ways, white was the opposite of red – where red is angry, white is peaceful and calm. Sacred objects used in the temples were white, as were the priest's clothing and sandals.

Undyed linen was often used for clothing, and therefore also depicted as white in artwork. The holy city Memphis was called Ineb Hedj, which meant White Walls. The color of Nefer – the crown of Upper Egypt – was also white.

Black (Kem)

Egypt was sometimes called Kemet, which meant the Black Land. As in modern, western civilization, black was a symbol of death, afterlife, and the night. But that concept was also coupled with the idea of resurrection. With death came resurrection and rebirth. So black was also a symbol of fertility and life. This idea likely came from the black soil surrounding the Nile, without which life in Ancient Egypt would have been all but impossible.

Anubis was the original god of the dead and was often depicted as a black jackal. And Queen Ahmose-Nefertari was the patroness of necropolis.

Yellow (Khenet)

Yellow was the color of the sun and gold. It was imperishable, eternal, and indestructible. The gods had both skin and bones of gold, since they were all but invulnerable. The Pharaohs were buried in golden sarcophagi, which signified that the Pharaoh had become a god.

Tutankhamun's mummy wore a solid gold mask and a gold Usekh (collar).

Blue (Irtiu)

Blue was the symbol of the sky and waters, of the heavens and primeval floods. It was also a symbol of life, rebirth, and fertility. This association probably originated with the Nile River, which brought fertility to the Egyptian soil.

The god Thoth was often depicted as a man with the head of either a baboon or an ibis (a blue bird). He was the god of secrets, arbitration, and the judgment of the dead. He also was credited with bringing humanity the writing system, science, and the arts of magic.

The Bennu bird – probably the predecessor of the Greek phoenix – symbolized the Nile's annual flooding. This heron-like bird was often depicted with bright blue feathers to emphasize the connection with the rebirth of the lands.

In this book, I have designed two shawls in each of the six main colors, drawing inspiration from their meaning in ancient Egyptian myths.

Lace and Color

When knitting lace patterns, it is important to decide what you want to emphasize in the finished project. Usually you want the lace patterns to show clearly in the finished object, and not have the yarn's color changes compete for visual attention. If you choose to work your project in a variegated colorway, consider that the eye will be drawn to the color changes and away from the lace pattern. However, with a more solid color, the eye will be drawn towards the lace motifs. In this book, all of the colorways used are either solid or semi-solid. That's not to say that the individual knitter cannot substitute a more variegated colorway. In the end, the most important thing when choosing a color is that it's one that *you* like, since the finished shawl will be *yours*.

Color as Design Inspiration

When designing lace patterns (or any pattern for that matter), color is an important part of my inspiration. Many of my designs start with the yarn. I find some beautiful yarn and then try to associate it with something that will become part of the theme of the shawl. I often associate freely, but there is no denying that blue often makes me think of water, green of foliage, and red perhaps of fire and flames. And from that idea I begin to look for stories that I can tell with my shawl design. For example, I could start with a green skein of yarn and think that it would be lovely to design a shawl with leaves on it. Perhaps I can draw on a story, like the great world tree Yggdrasil in Norse mythology. If I then go and read a couple of stories about Yggdrasil, I find that it holds the nine worlds – three worlds above the earth (in heaven), three worlds on earth, and three worlds below the earth (in the underworld), and that there is a squirrel named Ratatosk that runs across the tree carrying messages between an eagle perched on the high branches of the tree to a wyrm dwelling beneath its roots. I could then use that idea to design a shawl in nine sections, one for each world, drawing on readings about each world to find an appropriate stitch pattern to represent each world. And if I wanted to get really fancy, I could try to add a stylized squirrel to the design, hiding somewhere.

This part of the design phase is a lot of fun, because you can really let your imagination run wild. There is nothing stopping you from associating freely and coming up with new ideas.

Sometimes the design inspiration starts with a story or something I've seen, and then there is a quest to find the perfect yarn and color to fit the design I have in mind. Often that's harder, but with the help of the internet and all the online yarn stores available, there is bound to be something available.

Ancient Egypt in Lace and Color began with the idea of color used in ancient Egypt – and in particular the symbolic meanings of the six main colors. The first step was to do some research into what these colors meant. And then once I had a general idea of their connotations, I tried to find stories or attributes that would fit the color and could be used in the design. When researching green, I found that Osiris was often shown with green skin. So it seemed like a good idea to design a green Osiris shawl. I also found that the land of the blessed dead was known as the Fields of Malachite, and since malachite is green it was another good fit.

For approximately half of the shawls, I had the yarn before I knew what the exact theme of the shawl would be. In the case of the green shawls, I had the Cascade Lace in the color *Malachite* before deciding on the theme. The fit between malachite yarn and the Fields of Malachite was too good to pass up, and thus the Fields of Malachite shawl was born. The Osiris shawl started at the other end. I knew I wanted to design a green shawl with an Osiris theme. I settled on the story of how Seth killed his brother and the coffin containing Osiris drifted down the Nile and got stuck in a cedar tree. So the next step was to find a good cedar green. Cephalopod Yarns suggested their *Nebraska Conehead* colorway, which almost exactly matched my vision of the green tree.

All this is not to discourage anyone from choosing a different color when knitting these patterns. One of my favorite parts of Ravelry and the online knitting community is how easy it is to see the same shawl knit in many different colors and yarn, and how much the choice of color changes the shawl. I particularly love when people post their own interpretations and associations between the color and the theme of the shawl. For example, even though the Ra and Apep shawl is designed to look like a sun, and is knit in a sunshine yellow color, I could easily imagine the shawl in black (for when the sun doesn't shine during the night), or red from the battle between Ra and Apep. Or, consider the Memphis shawl. Here, it is white since the original name for Memphis meant White Walls, but one might argue that it should be the color of the desert instead.

I hope you will let color inspire you as much as it has inspired me.

OSIRIS

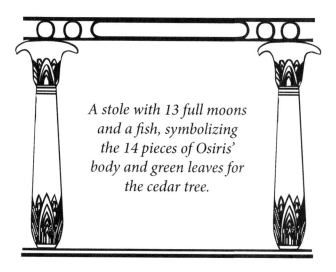

A stole with 13 full moons and a fish, symbolizing the 14 pieces of Osiris' body and green leaves for the cedar tree.

Osiris was the king of Egypt and Isis his queen. His brother Seth jealously plotted to overthrow him.

Osiris was generous in spirit and enjoyed hosting parties for the entire court. To one such soirée, Seth brought an exquisite wooden chest with gold decor. As the guests admired it, he promised to give it to the man who fit in it exactly. The guests were eager to try, but when they laid down in the chest, some were too short and others too tall. Seth knew that there was only one man who would be the right size for the chest, as he had already secretly acquired Osiris' measurements from his servant.

When all the guests had tried and failed, Osiris climbed in and was exactly the right size. As the guests laughed at Seth for losing such a valuable piece to his brother, Seth and his supporters suddenly slammed the lid on the chest, nailed it shut, and sealed it with molten lead so that Osiris died. The chest had been transformed into a coffin and Seth's supporters threw it in the Nile. Seth announced his brother's untimely death and declared himself King of Egypt.

Osiris' coffin drifted down the Nile and hit the shore close to a cedar tree. After searching for the coffin for days and nights, Isis found it and brought it

home. When Seth saw the coffin, he became very afraid. So one night he opened it, lifted out his brother's body and ripped it into 14 pieces – one for each full moon during the year. He spread the pieces over Egypt, certain Isis would never be able to find them.

Isis set out again to find Osiris, and wandered Egypt for many years. Finally she had gathered 13 of the 14 pieces, but the last piece – the phallus – had been consumed by a fish. So she fashioned a phallus out of gold, and brought Osiris back to life using all the magic she knew. They spent one passionate night together, so that she could carry his child. After that, Osiris' body died, but his spirit lived on. Ra-Atum made Osiris the king of the dead.

MATERIALS
- 2 skeins Cephalopod Yarns Skinny Bugga! [80% merino, 10% nylon, 10% cashmere; 424 yds per 113 g] shown in *Nebraska Conehead*
- 1 40-in US 6 [4 mm] circular needle
- Large-eyed, blunt needle
- Cable needle
- Stitch marker

GAUGE
21 sts and 23 rows = 4 in [10 cm] in stockinette, blocked

FINISHED (BLOCKED) SIZE
Width: 14 in [36 cm] / Length: 95 in [241 cm]

INSTRUCTIONS
CO 64 sts using the cable cast on.
Work charts in order. (All rows are charted.)
Work Rows 1-8 once.
Work Rows 9-44 seven times.
Work Rows 45-114 once.
Work Rows 115-150 six times.
Work Rows 151-156 once.

FINISHING

BO as follows: K2, *return sts to left needle,
k2tog tbl, k1, rep from * until no unworked sts
remain. Sew in ends and block.

CHART A

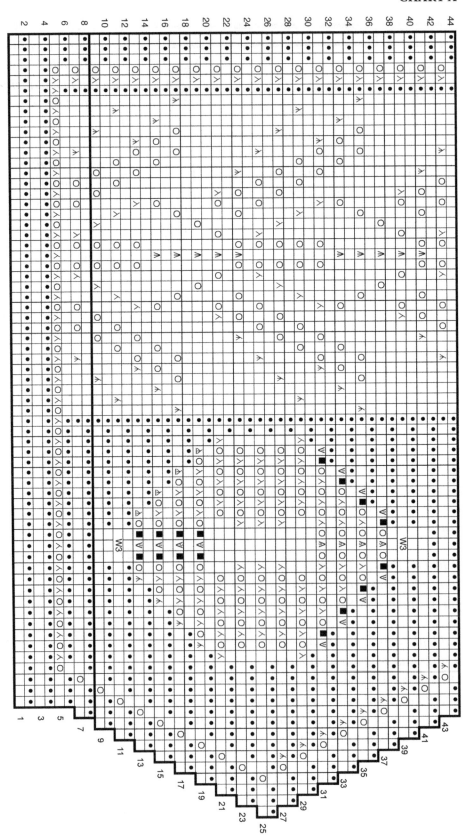

CHART B

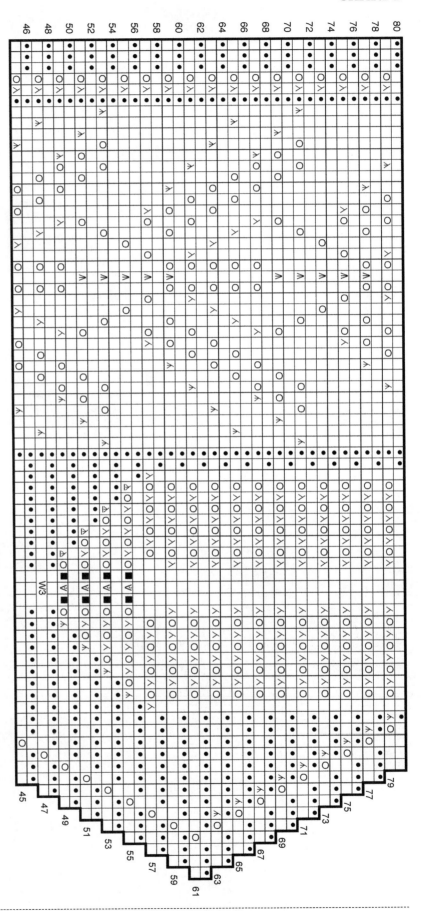

CHART C

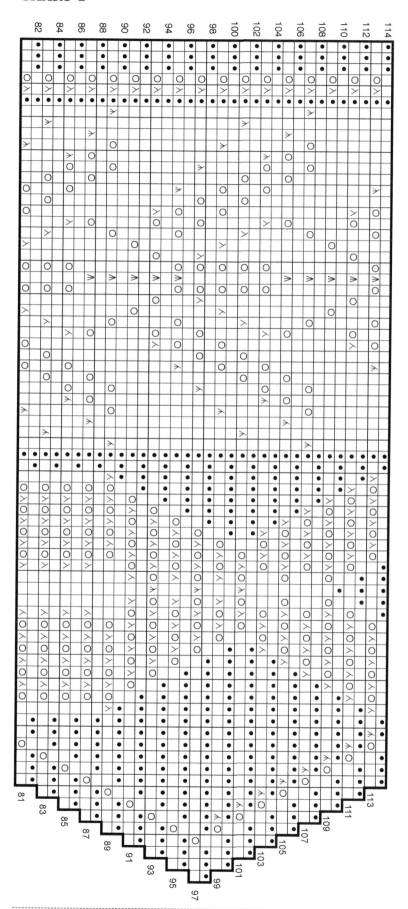

CHART D

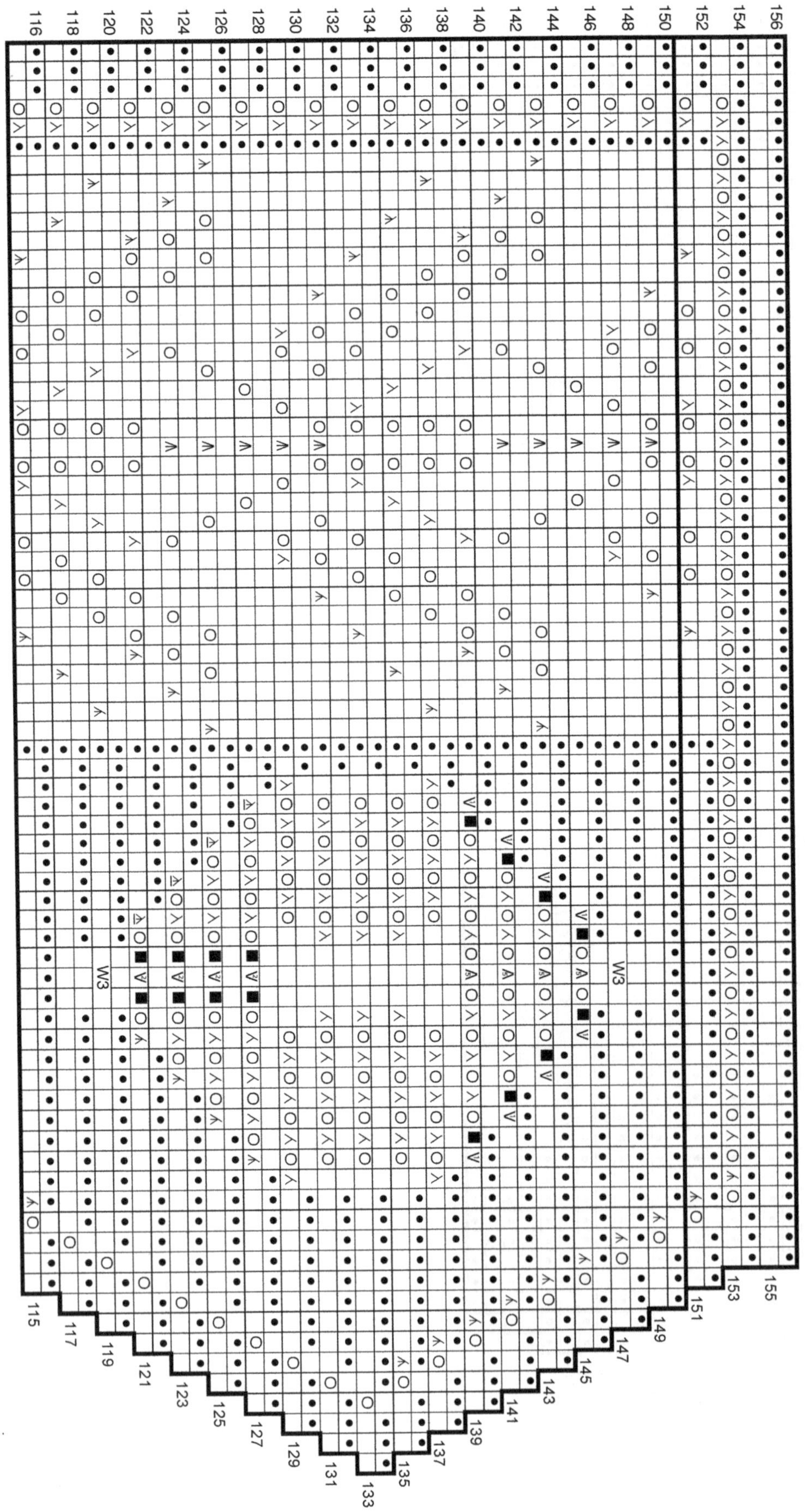

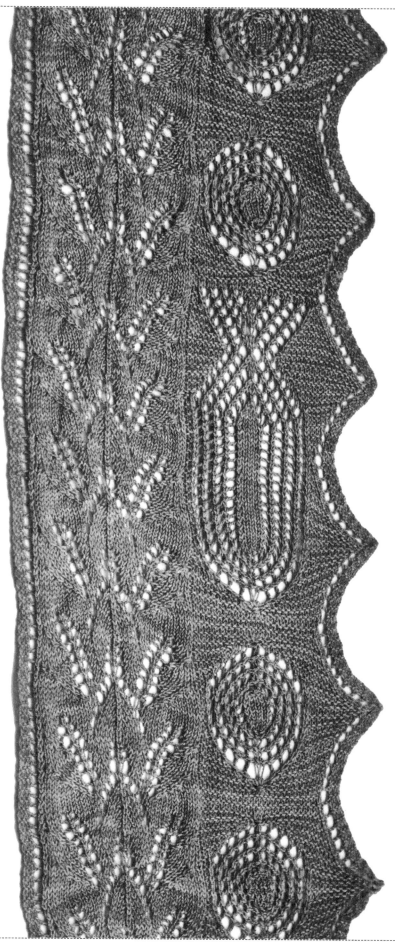

The photograph at left shows the fish motif near the center of this rectangular stole. The total shawl length is 95 in [241 cm], and altogether there are 13 moons surrounding the fish. Four moons are shown here.

FIELDS OF MALACHITE

A top-down, crescent-shaped shawl, showing stylized veins of malachite rock symbolizing the Fields of Malachite – the land of the blessed dead.

Osiris was the god of the dead, and it was believed that he could help the ancient Egyptians to the eternal paradise – life after death.

The land of the blessed dead was known as the Fields of Malachite, where conditions were remarkably similar to life on earth, except devoid of illness and other problems. In order to enter the Fields of Malachite, you had to convince Osiris that you were worthy. Worthiness meant balance rather than perfection, so the heart of the deceased would be weighed against the feather of Ma'at, and the person was expected to list all the evil acts they had not committed during their lifetime.

In addition, in order to guarantee a place in the Fields of Malachite, the body of the deceased had to be preserved during the burial, and the name of the deceased had to be inscribed in the pyramid and coffin, so the person would have a body and a name in the afterlife.

MATERIALS
➤ 1 skein Rocky Mountain Dyeworks Cascade Lace [50% silk, 50% merino wool; 400 yds per 90 g] shown in *Malachite*
➤ 1 40-in US 6 [4 mm] circular needle
➤ Large-eyed, blunt needle
➤ Stitch marker

GAUGE
16 sts and 24 rows = 4 in [10 cm] in stockinette, blocked

FINISHED (BLOCKED) SIZE
Wingspan: 63 in [160 cm] / Height: 26.5 in [67 cm]

INSTRUCTIONS
CO 5 sts using the cable cast on.
Set-up Row 1(RS): K2, PM, k3.
Set-up Row 2 (WS): K5.
Row 1: K2, yo, sl marker, k1, yo, k2 [7 sts].
Row 2: K2, p3, k2.
Row 3: K2, yo twice, knit to marker, yo, sl marker, k1, yo, knit to last 2 sts, yo twice, k2 [13 sts].
Row 4: K3, purl to last 3 sts, k3.
Rows 5-54: Repeat rows 3 & 4. At the end of row 54, there will be 163 sts.

Work charts in order. (All rows are charted.)
All RS rows: K2, chart A1 (or B1), k1, chart A2 (or B2), k2.
All WS rows: K2, chart A2 (or B2), p1, chart A1 (or B1), k2.

FINISHING
Row 101 (RS): K2, yo twice, (p1, ktbl) 6 times, yo, (p1, ktbl) 8 times, [p1, yo, (ktbl, p1) twice, (sl2 purlwise, sl1 knitwise, replace these 3 sts onto left needle, k3tog) once, (p1, ktbl) twice, yo, (p1, ktbl) 8 times] 4 times, p1, yo, (ktbl, p1) twice, (k5tog tbl) once, (p1, ktbl) twice, yo, p1, [(ktbl, p1) 8 times, yo, (ktbl, p1) twice, k3tog tbl, (p1, ktbl) 2 times, yo, p1] 4 times, (ktbl, p1) 8 times, yo, (ktbl, p1) 6 times, yo twice, k2 [303 sts].

Row 102: K3, p1, knit to the last 4 sts, p1, k3.
Rows 103-104: Knit.

BO as follows: K2, *return sts to left needle, k2tog tbl, k1, rep from * until no unworked sts remain. Sew in ends and block.

CHART A1

CHART A2

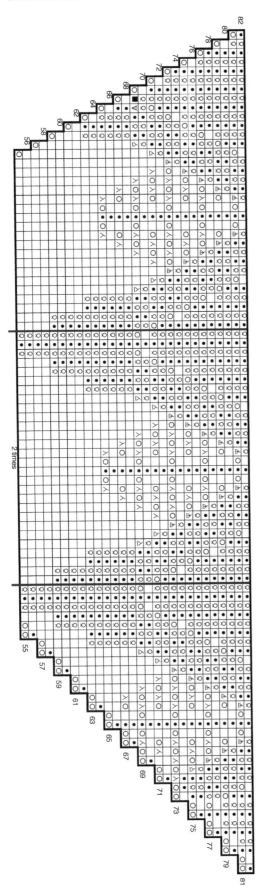

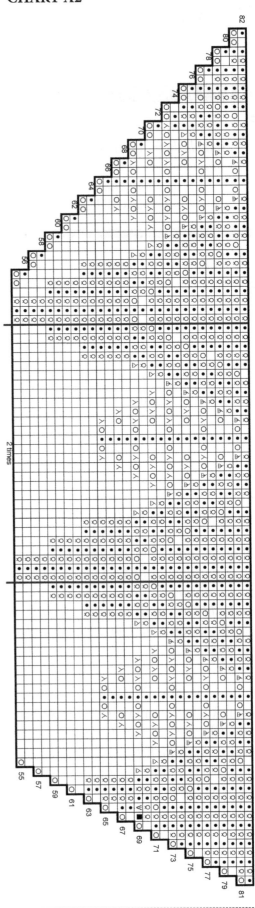

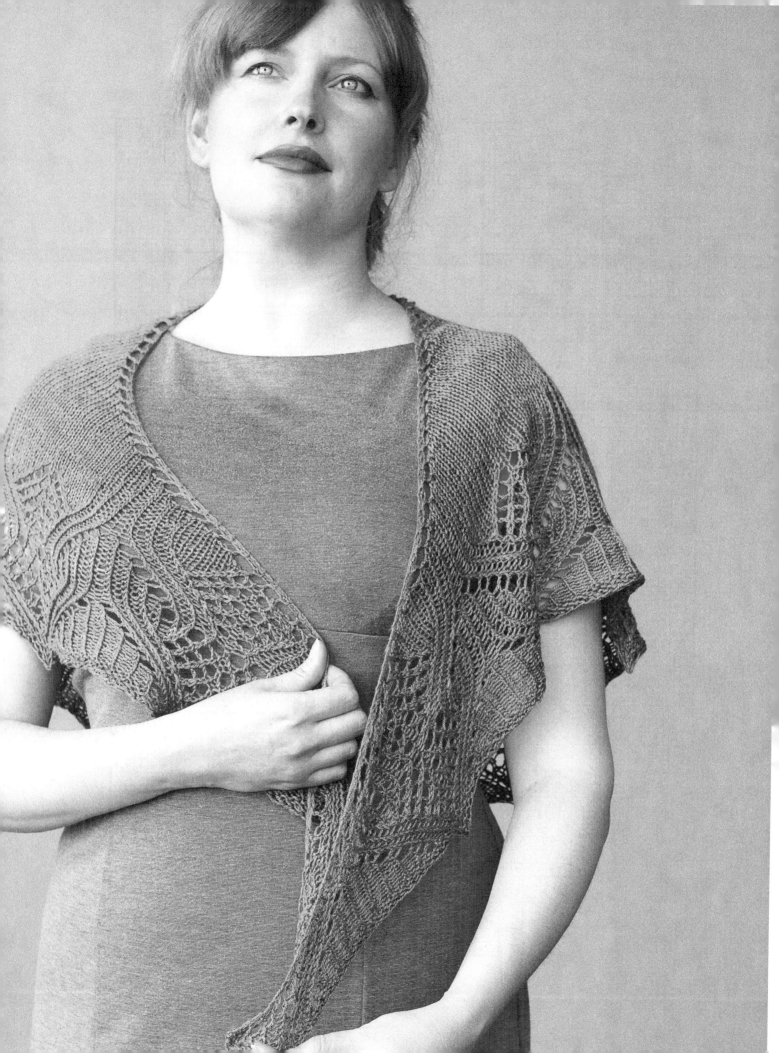

CHART B1

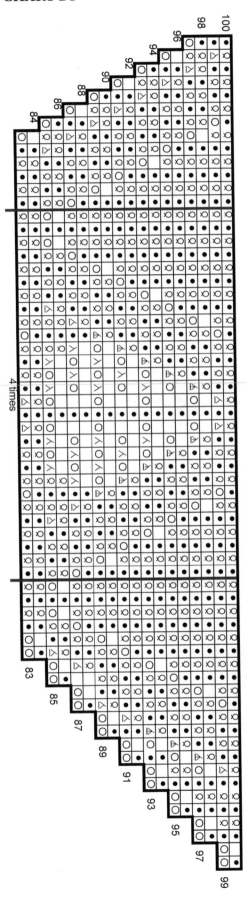

CHART B2

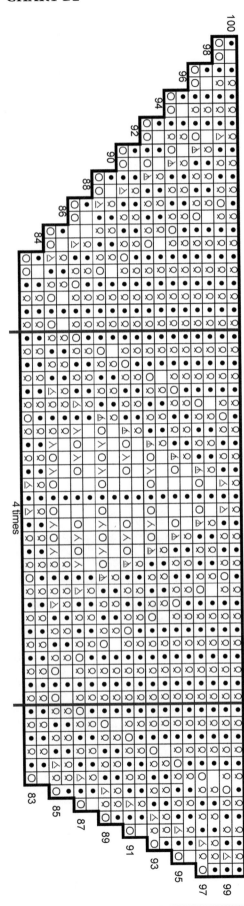

SETH

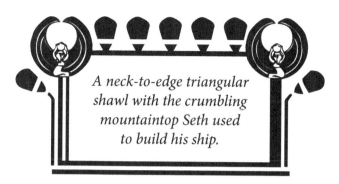

A neck-to-edge triangular shawl with the crumbling mountaintop Seth used to build his ship.

After killing his brother Osiris, Seth claimed Egypt's throne. But when Horus was old enough to challenge his uncle Seth, he gathered the other gods and told them of Osiris' murder.

To settle the dispute, Seth and Horus turned themselves into hippopotamuses and fought in the river. The one who broke the surface first would lose. Isis wished to help her son and threw a magic harpoon into the river, but in the fierce battle she couldn't tell who was who, and hit Horus instead. When he called out in pain, she withdrew the harpoon and threw it again and hit Seth. He cried out in pain and anger and broke the surface. Isis pitied him and let him go. Horus was furious that Isis had interfered, cut her head off with a copper knife, and stormed off. The other gods, angered that Horus had beheaded Isis, set out to search for him, while Isis transformed back to her usual self.

The Sun God ordered Horus and Seth to make peace with each other, but Seth suggested that they compete one last time. This time, they were each to build a stone ship and race down the Nile. The winner of the race would rule Egypt. The mighty Seth tore off a nearby mountaintop and dragged it down to the river. Horus' ship was already floating in the river, since he had secretly built a wooden ship and covered it in clay to so it would appear to be made of stone. When Seth put his ship in the river, it sank to the bottom. He then transformed himself into a hippopotamus and attacked Horus' ship. Since it was only made of wood, it splintered and sank, and that was the end of the race.

The gods were starting to despair that the case would never be settled. But finally the gods wrote a letter to Osiris himself. In reply, the king of the dead furiously demanded an explanation of why his son had been deprived the throne of Egypt. He threatened to send the demons of the underworld after the gods if Horus didn't get his throne.

Horus was crowned king of Egypt by the Sun God. The Sun God told Seth, "From now on, you will live with me in the heavens as the Lord of the Storms, and when you thunder, the whole world will tremble!" Finally, Seth was satisfied and made peace with Horus, and all the gods were happy.

MATERIALS
- 2 skeins The Verdant Gryphon Eidos [100% merino; 420 yds per 106 g] shown in *Charybdis*
- 1 40-in US 6 [4 mm] circular needle
- Large-eyed, blunt needle
- Stitch marker

GAUGE
18 sts and 28 rows = 4 in [10 cm] in stockinette, blocked

FINISHED (BLOCKED) SIZE
Wingspan: 74 in [188 cm] / Height: 37 in [94 cm]

INSTRUCTIONS
CO 7 sts using the cable cast on.
Set-up Row: Knit.
Work charts in order. (All rows are charted.)
All RS rows: K3, charted row, k1, charted row, k3.
All WS rows: K3, charted row, p1, charted row, k3.

FINISHING
BO as follows: K2, *return sts to left needle, k2tog tbl, k1, rep from * until no unworked sts remain. Sew in ends and block.

CHART A

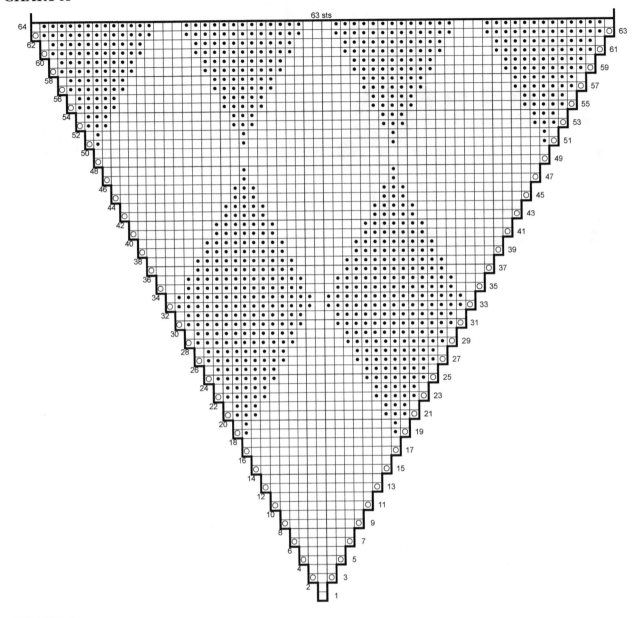

CHART B

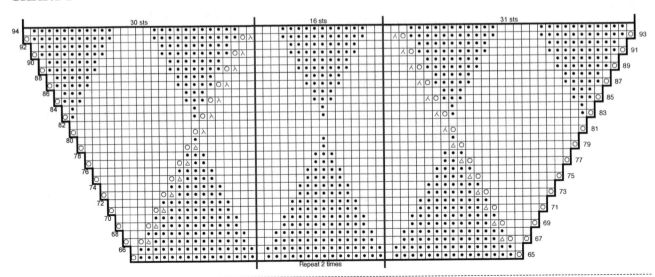

CHART C　　　　**CHART D**

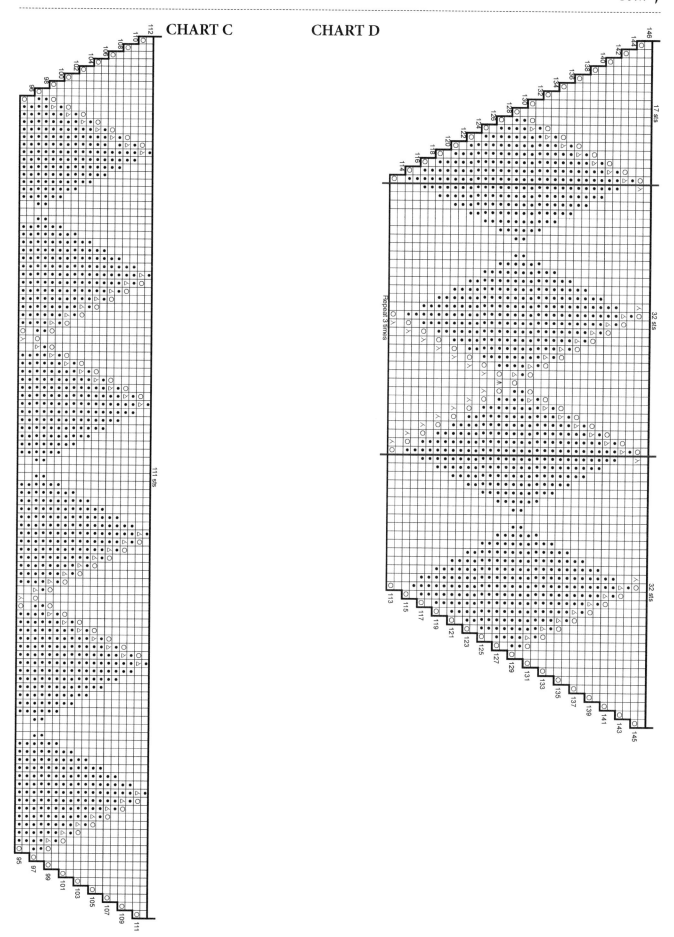

CHART E

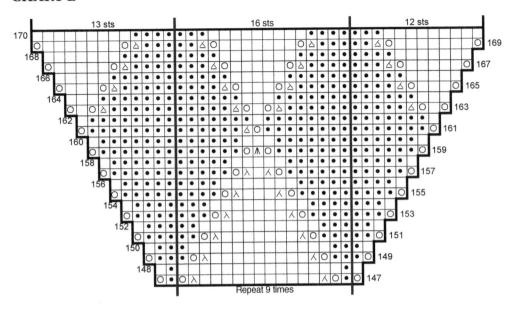

CHART F

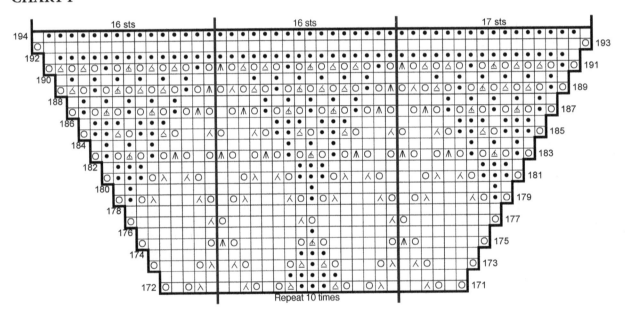

THE GIRL WITH THE ROSE RED SLIPPERS

A half-octagon, knit from neck to edge. Inspired by an Egyptian Cinderella story, this shawl shows the water and edge of the marble pool, the flowers of the garden, the tears spilled over the missing slipper, and the feathers of the eagle.

In the last days of ancient Egypt, a wealthy merchant was walking in the marketplace. As he passed by the slaves being sold, he saw a most beautiful girl among the slaves, so he purchased her. Her name was Rhodopis, and she had been taken from her home as a child by pirates and sold as a slave. The merchant soon became quite taken with her and spoiled her as if she were his own daughter. He gave her a house to live in, with a garden and slave girls to attend to her.

One day, as Rhodopis was bathing in the marble-edged pool in her garden, an eagle swooped down from the sky. The slave girls ran to hide among the flowers. The eagle picked up one of Rhodopis' rose red slippers in its talons, and flew away southwards over the Nile. The eagle may have been sent by the gods, and he flew straight to Memphis and swooped down over the palace and dropped the rose red slipper into Pharaoh Amasis' lap.

As Pharaoh Amasis picked up the little slipper, he admired the workmanship and was certain that the girl to whom it belonged must be one of the loveliest in the world. So he issued a decree and sent his messengers through the entire kingdom to find the girl whose foot the slipper came from. She would be the bride of Pharaoh.

The messengers travelled far and wide, and eventually came to the house of the wealthy merchant. When they showed Rhodopis the rose red slipper, she held out her foot so they could see how well it fitted her. And she sent one of the slave girls to fetch the matching slipper.

The messengers told Rhodopis that Pharaoh believed Horus had sent the eagle to him so that he would search for her. Rhodopis was brought to Memphis, and Pharaoh Amasis made her his Queen and the Royal Lady of Egypt. And they lived happily together for the rest of their lives.

MATERIALS

- 1 skein Rocky Mountain Dyeworks Glacier Ice Lace [70% baby alpaca, 30% silk; 875 yds per 100 g] shown in *Fireweed*
- 1 40-in US 2½ [3.0 mm] circular needle
- Large-eyed, blunt needle
- Stitch marker

GAUGE

21 sts and 29 rows = 4 in [10 cm] in pattern, blocked

FINISHED (BLOCKED) SIZE

Wingspan: 58 in [148 cm] / Height: 29 in [74 cm]

INSTRUCTIONS

CO 13 stitches.
Set-up Row 1 (RS): Knit.
Set-up Row 2 (WS): Knit.
Set-up Row 3: K3, yo, k1, M2, k1, M2, k1, M2, k1, yo, k3 [21 sts].
Set-up Row 4: k3, purl to last 3 sts, k3.

Then work the charts in order. (All rows are charted.) The charted row consists of the stitches between the bold lines.

Row 1 (RS): K3, charted row, k1, charted row, k1, charted row, k1, charted row, k3.

Row 2 (WS): K3, charted row, p1, charted row, p1, charted row, p1, charted row, k3.

Row 3: K3, yo, charted row, M2, charted row, M2, charted row, M2, charted row, yo, k3.

Row 4: As row 2.

FINISHING

Knit 3 rows.

Then BO as follows: k2, *return to left needle, k2tog tbl, k1, rep from * until no unworked sts remain.

Sew in ends and block.

CHART A

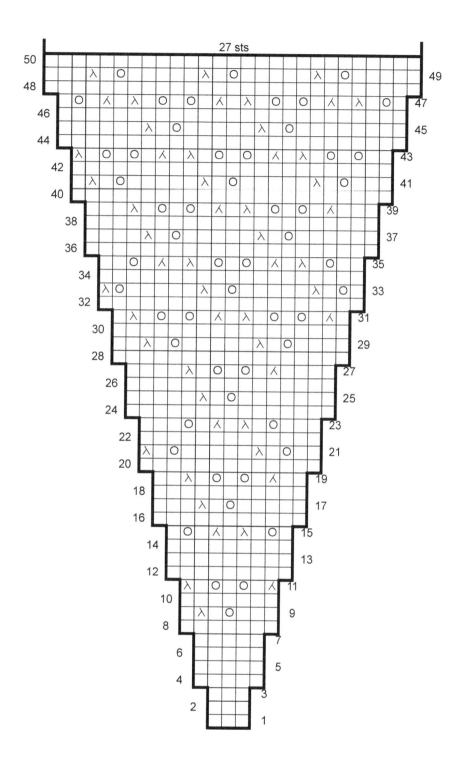

CHART B

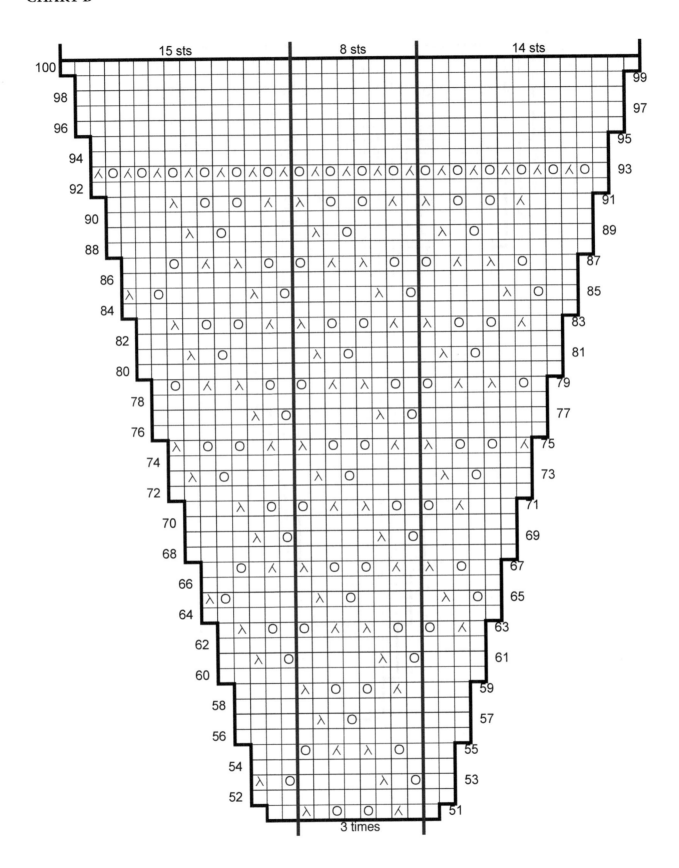

CHART C

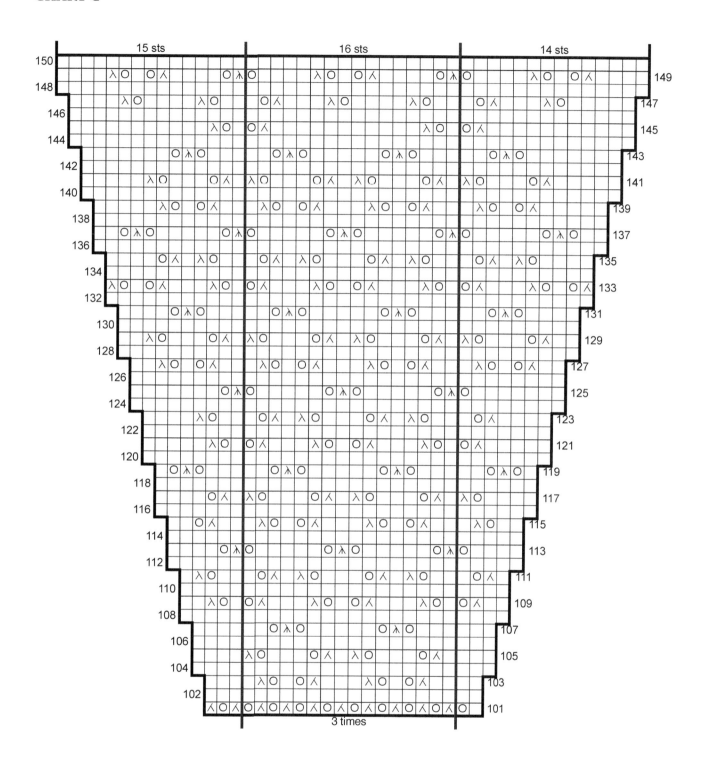

CHART D

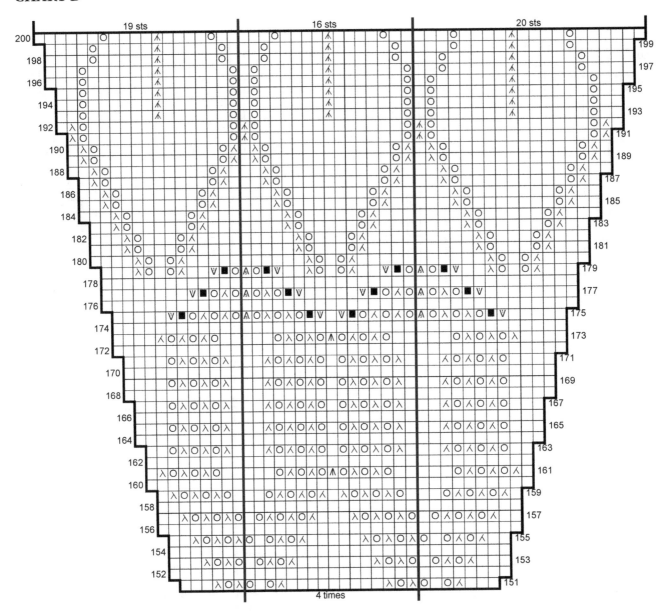

CHART E

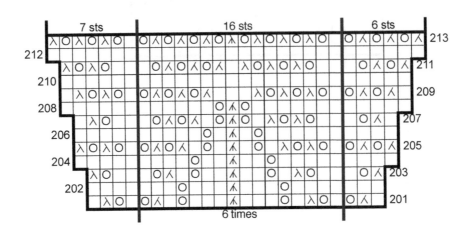

MEMPHIS

A circular pi shawl inspired by Ineb Hedj. The center symbolizes the walled city, surrounded by the desert. The outer portion contains a stylized version of the three great pyramids of Giza.

Memphis was the capital of ancient Egypt. The city was originally known as Ineb Hedj, which means White Walls. It is located south of Cairo, near the mouth of the Nile delta, and was founded by Pharaoh Menes around 3,000 BCE. It was a holy city, and was thought to be under the protection of the god Ptah, the patron of craftsmen.

Outside the city, in the desert, lay a royal necropolis and a number of pyramids. The largest were the three great pyramids of Giza, which belonged to the pharaohs Khufu, Khafra, and Menakure, who ruled during the fourth dynasty.

MATERIALS
- 1 skein Rocky Mountain Dyeworks Swiss Silk Lace [100% silk; 1000 yds per 100 g] shown in *Natural White*
- 1 32-in US 3 [3.25 mm] circular needle
- 1 set US 3 [3.25 mm] double-pointed needles
- Large-eyed, blunt needle
- Stitch marker

GAUGE
14 sts and 28 rows = 4 in [10 cm] in stockinette, blocked

FINISHED (BLOCKED) SIZE
Diameter: 52 in [132 cm]

INSTRUCTIONS
CO 9 sts using invisible loop cast on. (For tutorial, see http://techknitting.blogspot.com/2007/02/casting-on-from-middle-disappearing.html.) Divide evenly on 3 dpns. (Switch to circular needles when you have enough stitches on the needles, or use magic loop.)

Rnd 1: K9, mark beginning of round.
Rnd 2: [K1, yo] 9 times [18 sts].
Rnds 3-5: Knit.
Rnd 6: [K1, yo] 18 times [36 sts].
Rnd 7-12: Knit.
Rnd 13: [K1, yo] 36 times [72 sts].

Section 1
Work Chart A 12 times around. Even-numbered rnds are knit.

Rnd 27: [K1, yo] 72 times [144 sts].
Rnd 28: Knit.

Section 2
Work Chart B 6 times around. Even-numbered rnds are knit.

Rnd 53: [K1, yo] 144 times [288 sts].
Rnd 54: Knit.

Section 3
Work Chart C 12 times around. All rnds are charted.
Work rnds 58-65 FIVE times.

Rnd 103: [K1, yo] 288 times [576 sts].
Rnd 104: Knit.

Section 4

Work Chart D 6 times around. Then work Chart E
6 times around. All rnds are charted.

EDGING

Break the yarn.
CO 5 sts with a provisional cast on. Then work
Edging Chart.
At the end of row 1, k2tog the last stitch of the
edging with the first stitch of the shawl.
Work chart 47 times.
Each blue k2tog is to be worked together with the
next stitch from the main body of the shawl.

Work rows 1-23 of Edging Chart once more, then
graft together the last row with the provisional
cast-on edge.

FINISHING

Sew in ends and block.

CHART A

CHART B

CHART C

EDGING CHART

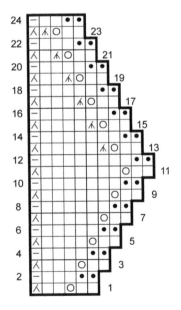

CHART D

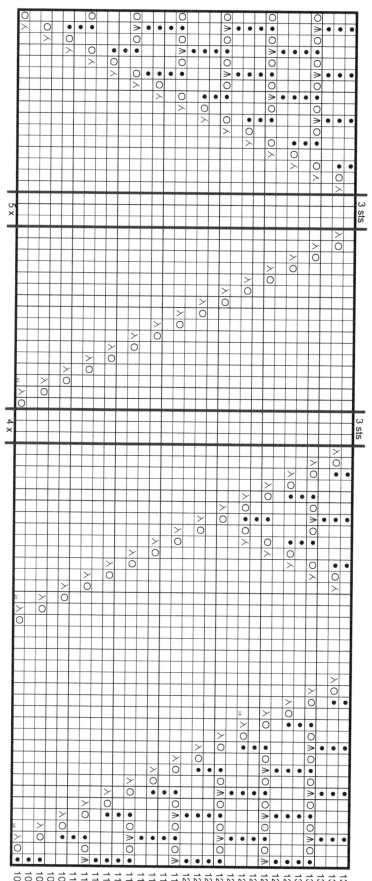

5 x

3 sts

4 x

3 sts

CHART E

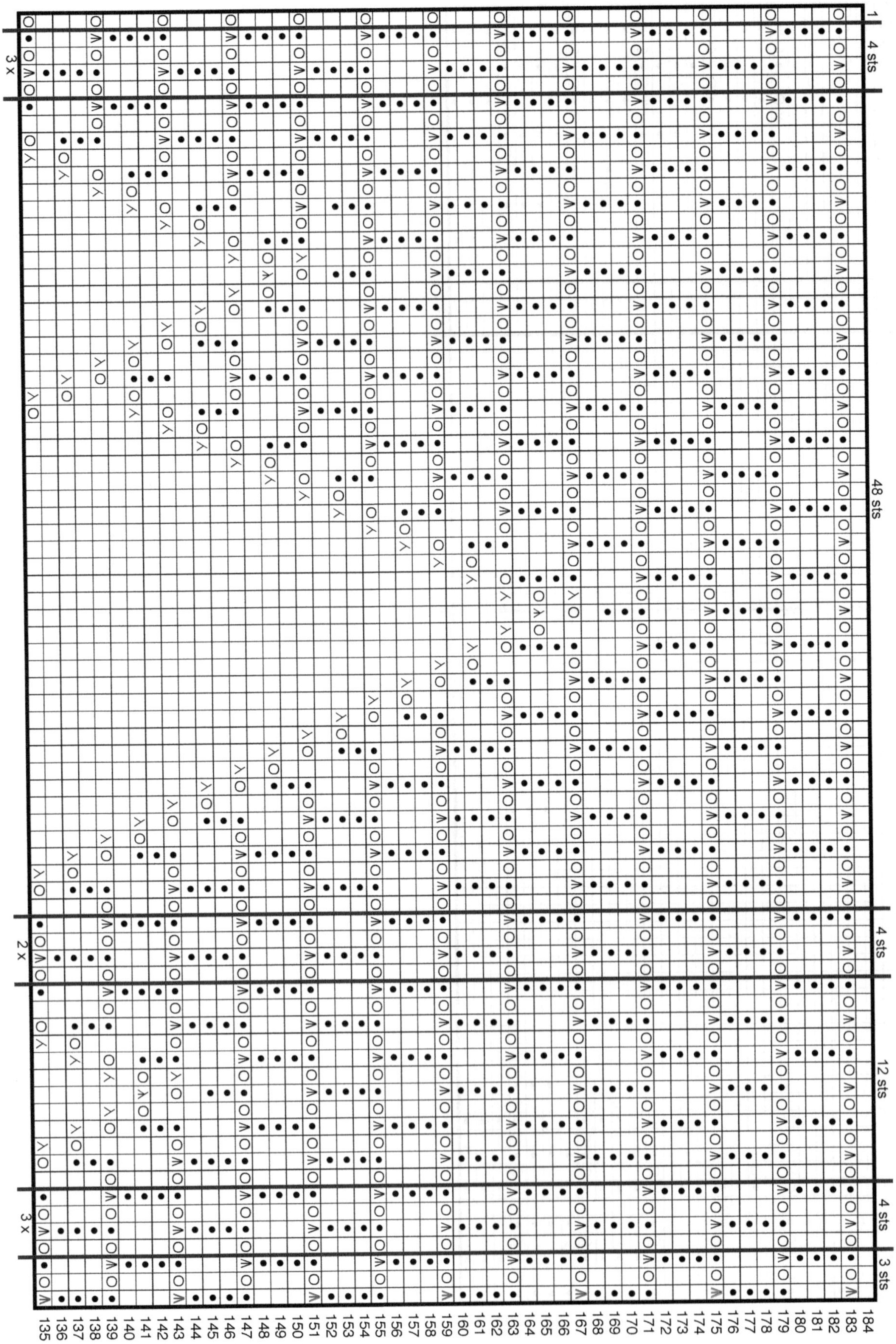
1
4 sts
48 sts
4 sts
12 sts
4 sts
3 sts
3 x
2 x
3 x
135 136 137 138 139 140 141 142 143 144 145 146 147 148 149 150 151 152 153 154 155 156 157 158 159 160 161 162 163 164 165 166 167 168 169 170 171 172 173 174 175 176 177 178 179 180 181 182 183 184

NEFER

A bottom-up, crescent-shaped shawl, with the beauty of Nefer. Knit in undyed Egyptian linen.

In the ancient Egyptian language Nefer meant beauty and goodness. The term can also refer to the white crown of Upper Egypt.

The nefer hieroglyph was used to decorate necklaces of particularly beautiful women, both in actual necklaces and artwork.

MATERIALS
- 2 (2) skeins Claudia Hand Painted Yarns Linen Lace [100% Egyptian linen; 540 yds per 100 g] shown in *Silver Shimmer*
- 1 40-in US 2½ [3.0 mm] circular needle
- Large-eyed, blunt needle
- Stitch marker

GAUGE
18.5 sts and 28 rows = 4 in [10 cm] in pattern, blocked

FINISHED (BLOCKED) SIZE
Smaller size: Wingspan: 52 in [132 cm] / Height: 15.5 in [40 cm]
Larger size: Wingspan: 58 in [147 cm] / Height: 17.5 in [44 cm]

INSTRUCTIONS
Cast on 389 (437) sts using the cable cast on and yarn held double. Cut off one of the strands of yarn. Continue knitting with one strand of yarn only.

Work Chart A, repeating center section 15 [17] times.
After row 46 on Chart A, there are 269 (301) sts.

Row 47: Yo, k2tog, k130 (146), charted row 47.

Then continue with chart B as written. Chart B is worked in short rows from the center of the shawl outward; turn at the end of each charted row.

Rows 53-60 are worked a total of 7 (8) times, each time adding 6 repeats of the section marked in red.
Then work rows 101-110 once, repeating the highlighted section 37 (42) times.

FINISHING
BO as follows: P2, *return to left needle, k2tog tbl, p1, rep from * until no unworked sts remain.
Sew in ends and block.

CHART A

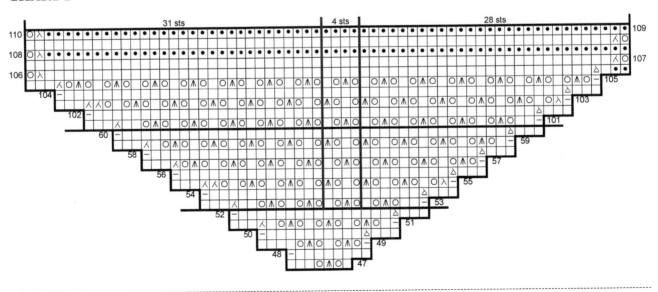

CHART B

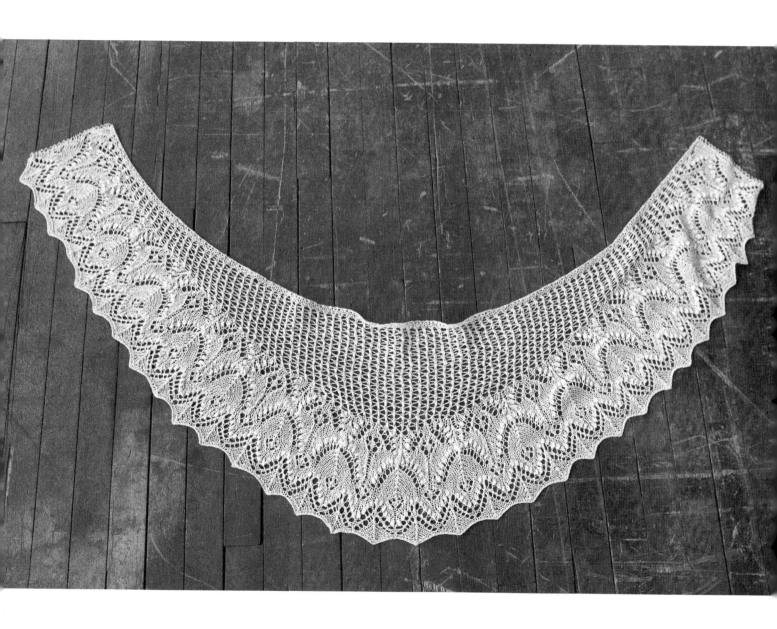

ANUBIS

A top-down, crescent-shaped shawl with the winding paths leading to the halls of Ma'at.

Before Osiris, Anubis was the god of the dead. Anubis is usually depicted as a man with a black jackal head.

Anubis would guide dead souls to Osiris and the halls of Ma'at where they would be judged. Anubis placed a dead soul's heart upon the Scales of Justice. If the heart was heavier than the feather of Ma'at because the person had failed to lead a balanced life, the soul was found guilty. Such souls would then be fed to Ammit – a demon with the head of a crocodile, the torso of a leopard, and the rear of a hippopotamus. But if found innocent, the soul would be led by Anubis to its heavenly home in the Fields of Malachite.

MATERIALS
- ❧ 1 skein Zen Yarn Garden Serenity Lace II [80% merino, 10% nylon, 10% cashmere; 575 yds per 115 g] shown in *Midnight Blue*
- ❧ 1 40-in US 6 [4 mm] circular needle
- ❧ Large-eyed, blunt needle
- ❧ Stitch marker

GAUGE
18 sts and 29 rows = 4 in [10 cm] in stockinette, blocked

FINISHED (BLOCKED) SIZE
Wingspan: 68 in [173 cm] / Height: 22 in [56 cm]

INSTRUCTIONS
CO 5 sts using the cable cast on.
Set-up Row 1 (RS): K2, PM, k3.
Set-up Row 2 (WS): K5.

Row 1: K2, yo, sl marker, k1, yo, k2 [7 sts].
Row 2: K2, p3, k2.
Row 3: K2, yo twice, knit to marker, yo, sl marker, k1, yo, knit to last 2 sts, yo twice, k2 [11 sts].
Row 4: K3, purl to last 3 sts, k3.
Rows 5-68: Repeat rows 3 & 4. At the end of row 68, there are 205 sts on the needles.

All RS rows: K2, chart A1, k1, chart A2, k2.
All WS rows: K3, purl to last 3 sts, k3.

FINISHING
Row 118-120: Knit.
BO as follows: K2, *return sts to left needle, k2tog tbl, k1, rep from * until no unworked sts remain. Sew in ends and block.

CHART A1

CHART A2

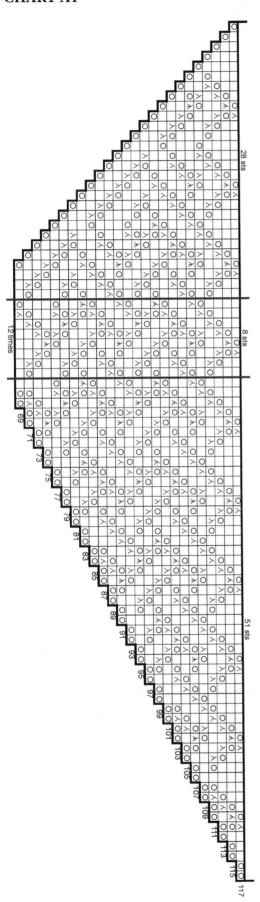

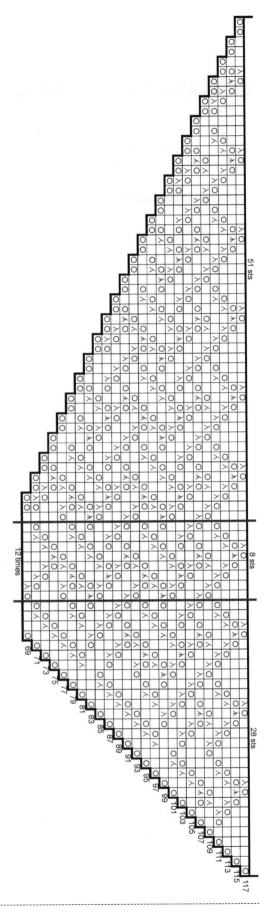

NEFERTARI

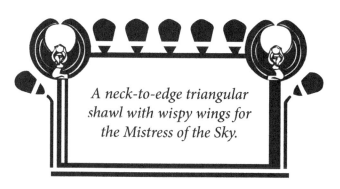

A neck-to-edge triangular shawl with wispy wings for the Mistress of the Sky.

Queen Nefertari is one of the best-known Egyptian queens and the most famous of Ramesses the Great's many wives. Upon her death, she became the patron deity of the Theban necropolis and was worshipped as a goddess in Thebes. Her tomb is one of the most beautiful in the Valley of Queens. She was known as the Lady of the West and the Mistress of the Sky.

MATERIALS
- 2 skeins Indigodragonfly Merino Silk 4 Ply Sock [50% silk, 50% superwash merino; 430 yds yds/393 m per 100 g] shown in *"Did I listen to pop music because I was miserable? Or was I miserable because I listened to pop music?"*
- 1 40-in US 6 [4.0 mm] circular needle
- Large-eyed, blunt needle
- Stitch marker

GAUGE
13 sts and 26 rows = 4 in [10 cm] in pattern, blocked

FINISHED (BLOCKED) SIZE
Wingspan: 90 in [228 cm] / Height: 45 in [114 cm]

INSTRUCTIONS
CO 5 sts.
Set-up Row 1: Knit.

Start working charts in order.
All RS rows: K2, charted row, k1, charted row, k2.
All WS rows: K2, charted row, p1, charted row, k2.

When working chart A, work rows 23-38 THREE times (or as many times as desired), each time adding 2 repeats of the stitches in the red box.

FINISHING
Knit 3 rows.
BO as follows: K2, *return to left needle, k2tog tbl, k1, rep from * until no unworked sts remain.
Sew in ends and block.

CHART A

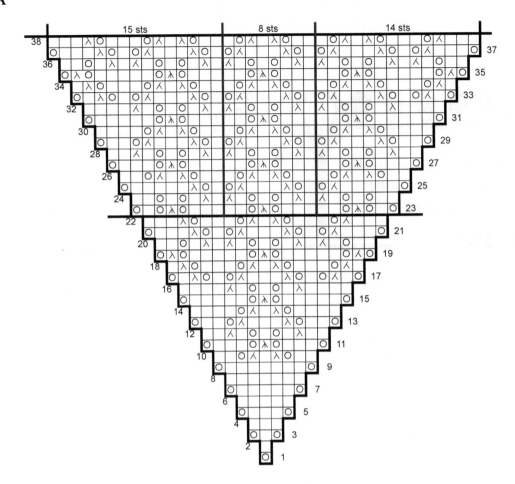

CHART B

On this and subsequent charts, repeat the stitches between the red lines as indicated in the chart.

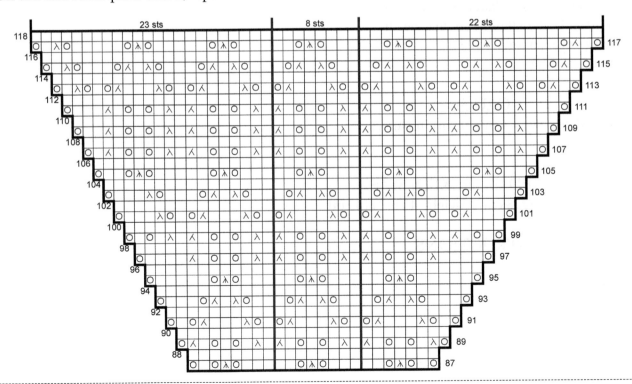

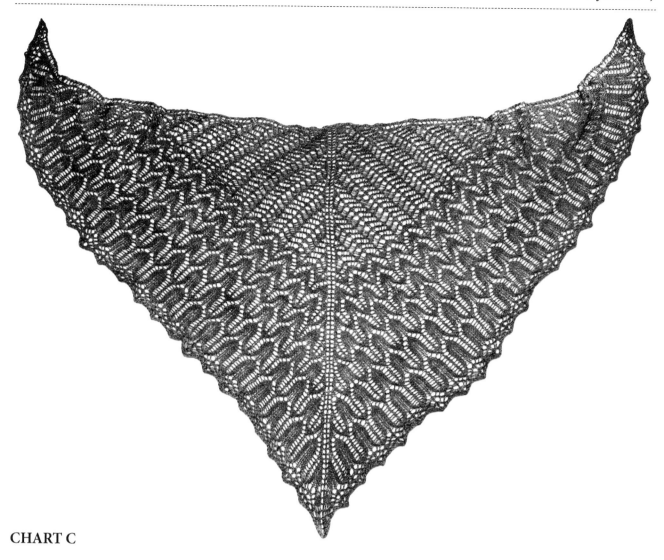

CHART C

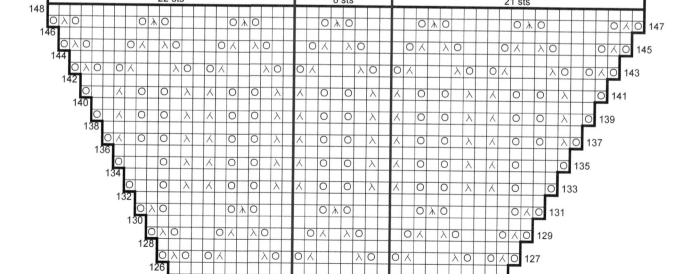

CHART D

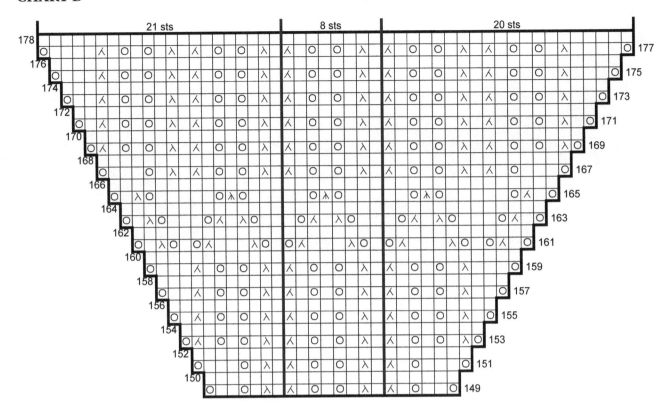

CHART E

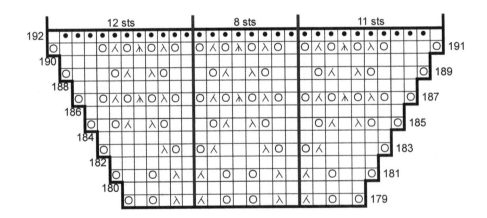

RA AND APEP

A circular pi shawl with a knit-on edging symbolizing the sun disk traveling across the sky.

Ra was the ancient Egyptian sun god, and he represented light, warmth, and growth. Apep was a demon from the underworld and took the form of a giant water snake.

Each day, Ra would carry the sun disk in his ship across the sky. And each night, the sun god had to travel through the underworld to return to the east. Apep knew which way Ra would have to travel in order to put the sun back into the sky. So every morning Apep would hide at the base of Bakhu the mountain of the horizon. Apep would try to defeat Ra to keep the sun from rising the next morning. If Apep succeeded, the world would be thrown into chaos. A few times, Apep did manage to swallow the sun boat, causing a solar eclipse, but inevitably Ra's supporters would free the sun by cutting a hole in Apep's belly and freeing the golden orb.

Eventually Apep was defeated. When Ra decapitated the snake, the red color in the sky during sunrise was thought to be Apep's blood.

MATERIALS

- 2 skeins Indigodragonfly MCN Lace [80% merino, 10% cashmere, 10% nylon; 575 yds per 115 g] shown in *What the Hay?*
- 1 32-in US 6 [4.0 mm] circular needle
- Large-eyed, blunt needle
- Stitch marker

GAUGE
14 sts and 27 rows = 4 in [10 cm] in pattern, blocked

FINISHED (BLOCKED) SIZE
Diameter (from center to outer "sun" point): 64 in [163 cm]

INSTRUCTIONS
CO 9 sts using invisible loop cast on (see http://techknitting.blogspot.com/2007/02/casting-on-from-middle-disappearing.html for tutorial). Divide evenly on 3 dpns (switch to circular needles when you have enough stitches on the needles, or use magic loop).

Rnd 1: K9, mark beginning of round.
Rnd 2: [K1, yo] 9 times [18 sts].
Rnds 3-5: Knit.
Rnd 6: [K1, yo] 18 times [36 sts].
Rnd 7-12: Knit.
Rnd 13: [K1, yo] 36 times [72 sts].
Note: All even rnds from this point are knit.

Section 1
Work Chart A 12 times around.
Rnd 27: [K1, yo] 72 times [144 sts].
Rnd 28: Knit.

Section 2
Work Chart B 12 times around.
Rnd 53: [K1, yo] 144 times [288 sts].
Rnd 54: Knit.

Section 3

Work Chart C 12 times around.
Rnd 103: [K1, yo] 288 times [576 sts].
Rnd 104: Knit.

Section 4

Work Chart D 12 times around.
Work Rnds 105-113 a total of 6 times.

EDGING

Break the yarn. CO 5 sts with a provisional cast on. At the end of each RS row, k2tog the last stitch of the edging with the next stitch of the shawl, starting with the first stitch of the round.

Work Edging Chart, working rows 1-98 TWELVE TIMES.
Graft rem 5 sts with the 5 sts from the provisional cast on.

FINISHING

Sew in ends and block.

CHART A

6 sts

25
23
21
19
17
15

CHART B

12 sts

51
49
47
45
43
41
39
37
35
33
31
29

CHART C

24 sts

101
99
97
95
93
91
89
87
85
83
81
79
77
75
73
71
69
67
65
63
61
59
57
55

CHART D

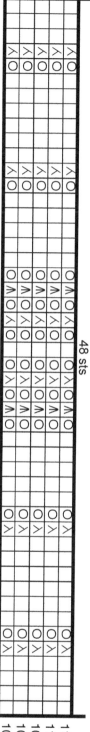

48 sts

105
107
109
111
113

EDGING CHART

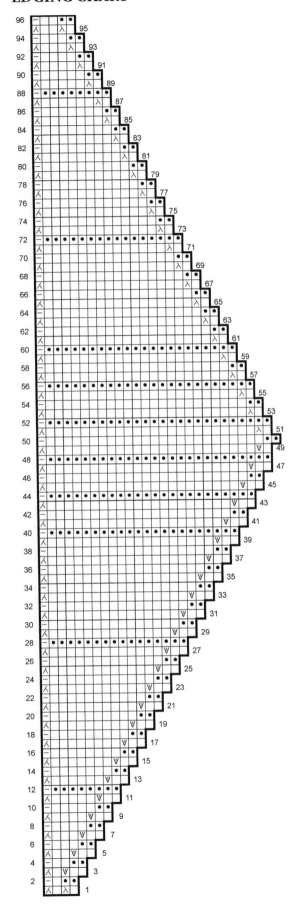

EGYPTIAN GOLD

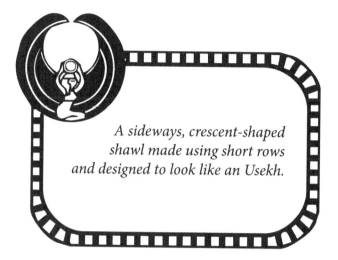

A sideways, crescent-shaped shawl made using short rows and designed to look like an Usekh.

Gold was thought to be a divine and indestructible substance. It was used to make jewelry as well as to cover statues of gods, tombs, and furniture of the Pharaohs. Since the dead were believed to bring their belongings to the next life, golden jewelry were buried with their owners.

The skin of the gods was thought to be made of gold. This led to the Egyptians covering the sarcophagus of Pharaohs upon their deaths, and Tutankhamun even wore a solid gold funeral mask, as well as an Usekh collar or necklace. The Usekh was draped around the neck and supported by the shoulders.

MATERIALS
- 1 skein Rocky Mountain Dyeworks Glacier Ice Lace [70% baby alpaca, 30% silk; 875 yds per 100 g] shown in *Egyptian Gold*
- 1 32-in US 1½ [2.5 mm] circular needle
- Large-eyed, blunt needle

GAUGE
25 sts and 52 rows = 4 in [10 cm] in pattern, blocked

FINISHED (BLOCKED) SIZE
Length: adjustable, shown as 36 in [91 cm] inner length / Width: 12 in [30 cm]

INSTRUCTIONS
CO 77 sts using the cable cast on and yarn held double. After casting on, cut off one of the strands of yarn, leaving enough length to weave in later. Continue knitting with one strand of yarn only.
Rows 1-8: [K1, p1] to last st, k1.

Then alternate working OPENWORK and SOLID GOLD sections as many times as desired, ending with an OPENWORK section. Then proceed to FINISHING.

OPENWORK
Row 1: [K1, p1] 6 times, [k2tog, yo, k1] 8 times, [k1, p1] 6 times, [k2tog, yo, k1] 8 times, k1, [p1, k1] 2 times.
Row 2: [K1, p1] 2 times, k1, [K2tog, yo, k1] 8 times, [p1, k1] 6 times, [k2tog, yo, k1] 8 times, [p1, k1] 6 times.
Row 3: [K1, p1] 6 times, [k2tog, yo, k1] 7 times, w&t.
Row 4: [K2tog, yo, k1] 7 times, [p1, k1] 6 times.
Row 5: [K1, p1] 6 times, [k2tog, yo, k1] 6 times, w&t.
Row 6: [K2tog, yo, k1] 6 times, [p1, k1] 6 times.
Row 7: [K1, p1] 6 times, [k2tog, yo, k1] 5 times, w&t.
Row 8: [K2tog, yo, k1] 5 times, [p1, k1] 6 times.

Row 9: [K1, p1] 6 times, [k2tog, yo, k1] 4 times, w&t.
Row 10: [K2tog, yo, k1] 4 times, [p1, k1] 6 times.
Row 11: [K1, p1] 6 times, [k2tog, yo, k1] 3 times, w&t.
Row 12: [K2tog, yo, k1] 3 times, [p1, k1] 6 times.
Row 13: [K1, p1] 6 times, [k2tog, yo, k1] 2 times, w&t.
Row 14: [K2tog, yo, k1] 2 times, [p1, k1] 6 times.
Row 15: [K1, p1] 6 times, [k2tog, yo, k1], w&t.
Row 16: [K2tog, yo, k1], [p1, k1] 6 times.

Row 17: [K1, p1] 24 times, [k2tog, yo, k1] 7 times, w&t.

Row 18: [K2tog, yo, k1] 7 times, [p1, k1] 24 times.

Row 19: [K1, p1] 24 times, [k2tog, yo, k1] 6 times, w&t.

Row 20: [K2tog, yo, k1] 6 times, [p1, k1] 24 times.

Row 21: [K1, p1] 24 times, [k2tog, yo, k1] 5 times, w&t.

Row 22: [K2tog, yo, k1] 5 times, [p1, k1] 24 times.

Row 23: [K1, p1] 24 times, [k2tog, yo, k1] 4 times, w&t.

Row 24: [K2tog, yo, k1] 4 times, [p1, k1] 24 times.

Row 25: [K1, p1] 24 times, [k2tog, yo, k1] 3 times, w&t.

Row 26: [K2tog, yo, k1] 3 times, [p1, k1] 24 times.

Row 27: [K1, p1] 24 times, [k2tog, yo, k1] 2 times, w&t.

Row 28: [K2tog, yo, k1] 2 times, [p1, k1] 24 times.

Row 29: [K1, p1] 24 times, [k2tog, yo, k1], w&t.

Row 30: [K2tog, yo, k1], [p1, k1] 24 times.

Row 31: [K1, p1] 6 times, [k2tog, yo, k1] 8 times, w&t.

Row 32: [K2tog, yo, k1] 8 times, [p1, k1] 6 times.

Row 33-46: As rows 3-16.

SOLID GOLD

Row 1-8: [K1, p1] to last st, k1.

Row 9: [K1, p1] 36 times, k1, w&t.

Row 10: K1, [p1, k1] 36 times.

Row 11: [K1, p1] 33 times, k1, w&t.

Row 12: K1, [p1, k1] 33 times.

Row 13: [K1, p1] 30 times, k1, w&t.

Row 14: K1, [p1, k1] 30 times.

FINISHING

Row 1-8: [K1, p1] to last st, k1.

BO as follows: K2, *return sts to left needle, k2tog tbl, k1, rep from * until no unworked sts remain. Sew in ends and block.

BENNU

A semi-circular pi shawl with knit-on edging, stylized sun disks (diamonds), and Bennu feathers.

The ancient Egyptians linked the myth of the phoenix with immortality. According to legend, the Bennu bird created itself from a fire in a holy tree in the temple of Ra. The Egyptians considered this bird's rise from the ashes to be symbolic of the Nile river's annual flooding, which left the soil fertile again for the next farming season.

The Bennu bird had two long feathers on its crest and was often depicted with the sun disk crowning its head.

MATERIALS
- 1 skein Rocky Mountain Dyeworks Emerald Lake Lace [80% merino, 20% silk; 1275 yds per 105 g] shown in *Lapis Lazul*
- 1 40-in US 5 [3.75 mm] circular needle
- Large-eyed, blunt needle
- Stitch marker

GAUGE
19 sts and 27 rows = 4 in [10 cm] in pattern, blocked

FINISHED (BLOCKED) SIZE
Radius: 36 in [91 cm]

INSTRUCTIONS
CO 4 sts using the knitted cast on.
Set-up Row 1: K1, kfb, kfb, k1 [6 sts].
Set-up Row 2: K1, kfb 4 times, k1 [10 sts].
Set-up Row 3: K3, p4, k3.

Row 1: K3, yo, [k1, yo] 4 times, k3 [15 sts].
Row 2: K3, p9, k3.
Row 3: Knit.
Row 4: K3, p9, k3.
Row 5: K3, [k1, yo] 9 times, k3 [24 sts].
Row 6 (and all subsequent WS rows): K3, purl to last 3 sts, k3.
Row 7: Knit.
Row 8: As row 6.
Rows 9-12: Work rows 7 & 8 twice more.
Row 13: K3, [k1, yo] 18 times, k3 [42 sts].
Row 14: K3, purl to the last 3 sts, k3.

Begin working charts in order. For all charts, RS rows are as charted; WS rows are: K3, purl to last 3 sts, k3.

Section 1
Work Chart A.
Row 27: K3, [k1, yo] 36 times, k3 [78 sts].
Row 28: K3, purl to last 3 sts, k3.

Section 2
Work Chart B.
Row 53: K3, [k1, yo] 72 times, k3 [150 sts].
Row 54: K3, purl to last 3 sts, k3.

Section 3
Work Chart C.
Row 103: K3, [yo, k1] 144 times, k3 [294 sts].
Row 104: K3, purl to last 3 sts, k3.

Section 4
Work Chart D.
Row 201: K3, [k1, yo] 288 times, k3 [582 sts].
Row 202: k3, purl to last 3 sts, k3.

EDGING

CO 18 sts using knitted cast on.
Set-up Row 1 (RS): K17, k2tog last stitch with first stitch on the body of the shawl.
Set-up Row 2 (WS): Sl1, purl to last 3 sts, k3.
Work both set-up rows once more, then work Edging Chart.

Work rows 1-48 TWENTY FOUR times.
Then work charted rows 1-2 ONCE more.

Finish edging:
Row 1 (RS): K17, k2tog last stitch with the next stitch on the body of the shawl.
Row 2 (WS): Sl1, purl to last 3 sts, k3.

Work Rows 1-2 one more time, then BO as follows: K2, *return to left needle, k2tog tbl, k1, rep from * until no unworked sts remain.

FINISHING

Sew in ends and block.

CHART A

3 sts	6 sts	3 sts	
	λ O		25
	λ O λ O		23
	λ O λ O λ O		21
	λ O λ O		19
	λ O		17
	● ● ● ● ● ●		15

6 times

CHART B

3 sts	12 sts	3 sts	
	λ O		51
	λ O λ O		49
	λ O λ O λ O		47
	λ O λ O λ O λ O		45
	λ O λ O λ O λ O λ O		43
	λ O λ O λ O λ O λ O λ O		41
	λ O λ O λ O λ O λ O		39
	λ O λ O λ O λ O		37
	λ O λ O λ O		35
	λ O λ O		33
	λ O		31
	● ● ● ● ● ● ● ● ● ● ● ●		29

Repeat 6 times

CHART C

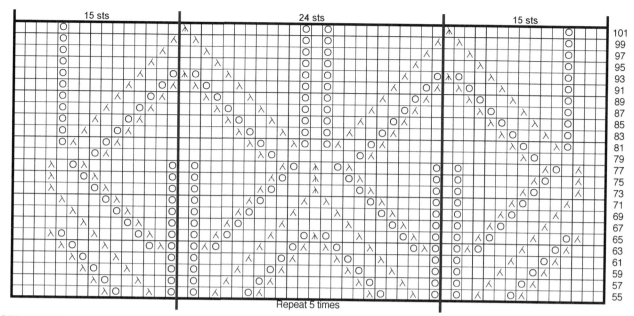

CHART D

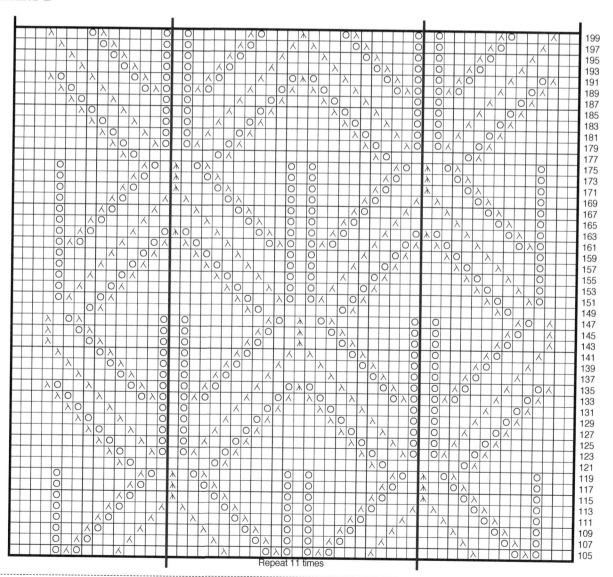

EDGING CHART

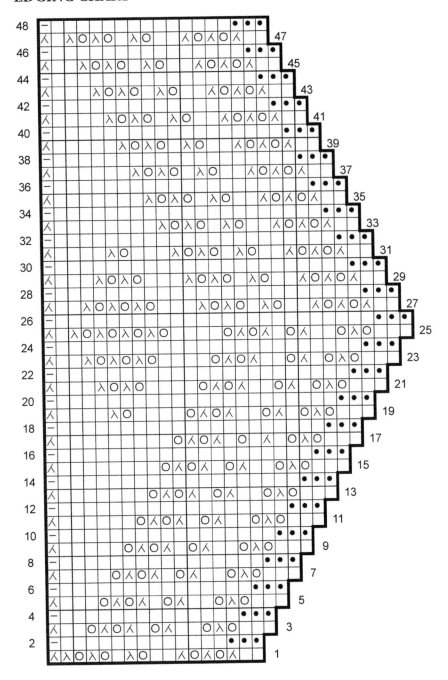

THOTH

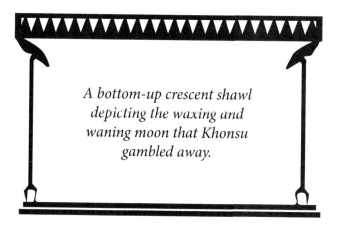

A bottom-up crescent shawl depicting the waxing and waning moon that Khonsu gambled away.

A long time ago, the moon was as bright as the sun, and it did not change from night to night. The moon god Khonsu was responsible for holding the moon up over Egypt. Every night he travelled with the moon across the sky. But even the bright moonlight had limits, and there were shadows that the light could not reach. Khonsu wanted to know what secrets were hiding in the shadows.

Thoth could see into the hearts and souls of all men and knew all their secrets. So Khonsu approached him and challenged him to a game of Senet. Khonsu asked Thoth to wager his secret knowledge in the game. In return, Khonsu would bet part of the moon's light.

Senet is a game of strategy, and both Khonsu and Thoth were very skilled players. The game went on for many hours, but in the end Thoth prevailed and defeated Khonsu.

Ever since then, Khonsu has not been able to show all the light of the moon. Every night, it gets a little brighter, until it reaches its full light, but then it grows dimmer again, as the light transfers to Thoth.

MATERIALS
- 1 skein The Verdant Gryphon Mithril Lace [100% merino; 750 yds per 106 g] shown in *Starry Night Over the Rhone*
- 1 40-in US 6 [4.0 mm] circular needles
- Large-eyed, blunt needle
- Stitch marker

GAUGE
15.5 sts and 36 rows = 4 in [10 cm] in pattern, blocked

FINISHED (BLOCKED) SIZE
Wingspan: 62 in [158 cm] / Height: 14 in [36 cm]

INSTRUCTIONS
CO 393 sts, using the cable cast on and yarn held double. After casting on, cut off one of the strands of yarn. Continue knitting with one strand of yarn only.

Work Chart A. After row 38 on Chart A, there are 267 sts.

Remainder of shawl is worked in short rows.
Row 39 (RS): K3, p1, k4, k130. Turn work.
Row 40 (WS): Sl1, p8. Turn work.

Work Chart B. (Row 40 is shown on the chart for reference, but you continue with Row 41 after Row 40.)
Chart B is worked in short rows outward from the center of the shawl; turn at the end of each charted row.

Work Rows 45-46 a total of TWENTY-SEVEN times, each time adding a repeat of the section marked in red.
Then work rows 47-50 ONCE, repeating the highlighted section TWENTY-SEVEN times.

EDGING

Row 51: BO 2 sts, replace lone st on left needle, then CO 7 sts using the cable cast on.
Edge set-up row: k7, k2tog, turn the work.

Work Edging Chart perpendicular to the top edge of the shawl. Each k2tog at the end of rows 2 and 4 works together the last st on the row with a stitch from the top edge of the shawl.

Repeat until no sts remain from body of shawl. Then turn and BO rem 8 sts as follows: K2, *return to left needle, k2tog tbl, k1, rep from * until no unworked sts remain.

FINISHING

Sew in ends and block.

CHART A

This chart is continued on page 79. Repeat red section FOUR times on each row.

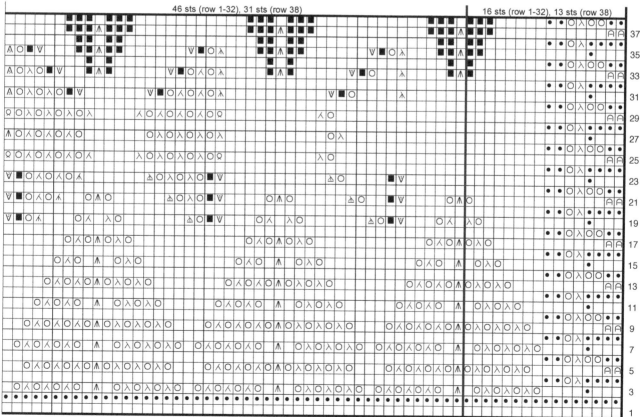

CHART B

EDGING CHART

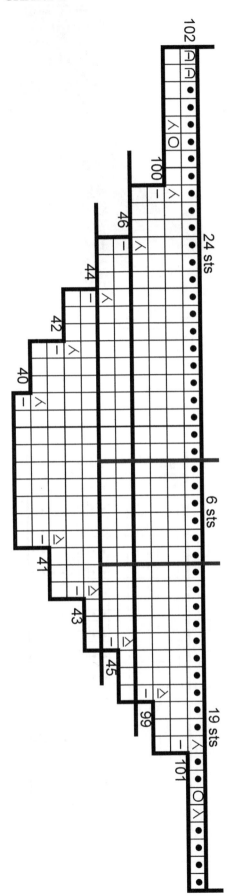

ABBREVIATIONS & TECHNIQUES

BO	bind off
CO	cast on
k	knit
kfb	knit into the front and back of the next stitch
ktbl	knit through the back loop
k2tog	knit two stitches together
k3tog	knit three stitches together
p	purl
p2tog	purl two stitches together
p3tog	purl three stitches together
PM	place marker
ptbl	purl through the back loop
psso	pass slipped stitch(es) over
rnd	round
RS	right side
sl	slip
ssk	slip slip knit (see right)
ssp	slip slip purl (see right)
st(s)	stitch(es)
tbl	through the back loop
w&t	wrap and turn
WS	wrong side
yo	yarn over

M2: [K, yo, k] into the same stitch.

nupp over 7 stitches: [K, yo] 3 times, k all into the same stitch. Note: All 7 nupp stitches are purled together on the subsequent WS row.

ssk: Slip stitch as if to knit, slip stitch as if to knit, replace on left needle, and knit both stitches together through the back loop.

ssp: Slip stitch as if to knit, slip stitch as if to knit, replace on left needle and purl both stitches together through the back loop.

w&t (wrap and turn): Bring yarn to front as if about to purl, slip one stitch purlwise. Turn work. The yarn is now in back of work. Bring yarn to the front, slip one stitch back to right needle.

w3 (wrap 3): [K, p, k] onto cable needle. Pass yarn in front of all stitches and then behind all the stitches (you have now wrapped the yarn once around all the stitches). Wrap the yarn two more times around the stitches for a total of 3 wraps. Place wrapped stitches on the right-hand needle.

w5 (work 5): Work 5 sts together as follows: ssk, k3tog, pass previous stitch over (the one from the ssk).

CHART SYMBOLS

Symbols used frequently throughout the book are listed in the left-hand column. The right-hand column shows those symbols that have specific meanings within particular patterns.

☐	k on RS, p on WS
●	p on RS, k on WS
Ϙ	ktbl on RS, ptbl on WS
⋏	(symbol in black) k2tog on RS, p2tog on WS
⋏	(symbol in blue) k2tog: last stitch of edging with next stitch on body of shawl
λ	ssk on RS, ssp on WS
⋏	sl1, k2tog, psso
⋏	k3tog
⋀	slip 2 stitches together (knitwise), k, psso
V	kfb
V̈	M2 (see explanation on facing page)
A̋	w5 (see explanation on facing page)
⋒	nupp (see explanation on facing page)
⌒	bind off 1 stitch
—	slip 1
O	yarn over
■	no stitch

Fields of Malachite	
⊿	sl2 purlwise, sl1 knitwise, replace the 3 sts onto left needle, k3tog
◿	sl1 purlwise, sl1 knitwise, replace the 2 sts onto left needle, k2tog
◿	k2tog tbl
⊿	k3tog tbl
Girl with the Rose Red Slippers	
⊿	k3tog tbl
Memphis	
⋀	(symbol in blue) start round 1 stitch early, then work ⋀ (see explanation at left)
Osiris	
⊿	k3tog tbl
w3	wrap 3 (see explanation on facing page)
Seth	
◿	p2tog
⊿	p3tog
◿	ssp
Thoth	
⊿	k3tog tbl
◿	p2tog on WS

YARNS USED

Cephalopod Yarns
Skinny Bugga!

Claudia Hand Painted Yarns
Linen Lace

Indigodragonfly
Merino Silk 4 Ply
MCN Lace

Rocky Mountain Dyeworks
Emerald Lake Lace
Glacier Ice Lace
Cascade Lace
Swiss Silk

The Verdant Gryphon
Eidos
Mithril Lace

Zen Yarn Garden
Serenity Lace II

Available from
Cephalopod Yarns, *cephalopodyarns.com*
Claudia Hand Painted Yarns, *claudiaco.com*
Indigodragonfly, *indigodragonfly.ca*
Rocky Mountain Dyeworks, *rockymountaindyeworks.com*
The Verdant Gryphon, *verdantgryphon.com*
Zen Yarn Garden, *zenyarngarden.com*

FURTHER READING

Brier, Bob, and Hoyt Hobbs. *Daily Life of the Ancient Egyptians.* 2nd ed. Greenwood Press, 2008.

David, Rosalie. *Religion and Magic in Ancient Egypt.* Penguin, 2003.

Harris, Geraldine. *Gods and Pharaohs from Egyptian Mythology.* Peter Bedrick Books, 1996.

Mertz, Barbara. *Red Land, Black Land: Daily Life in Ancient Egypt.* HarperCollins, 2008.

Mertz, Barbara. *Temples, Tombs, and Hieroglyphs: A Popular History of Ancient Egypt.* 2nd ed. William Morrow, 2007.

Millmore, Mark. Discovering Ancient Egypt website. http://www.discoveringegypt.com/.

Owusu, Heike. *Egyptian Symbols.* Sterling Publishing, 1998.

Patch, Diana Craig. *The Dawn of Egyptian Art.* Metropolitan Museum of Art, 2012.

Pinch, Geraldine. *Egyptian Mythology: A Guide to the Gods, Goddesses, and Traditions of Ancient Egypt.* Oxford University Press, 2004.

ABOUT ANNA DALVI

Anna Dalvi has been publishing knitting patterns online since 2007. She has self-published more than 70 patterns over the past several years. Her most popular designs are the Mystic lace shawls, originally published in a mystery knitalong format, which have attracted more than 7,000 knitters worldwide. This is her second book with lace designs, following *Shaping Shawls* (2011). Her website has had 120,000 readers in the past year, and the readership grows annually.

In her knitting, Anna enjoys variety more than anything else — from intricate lace to sprawling cables, and differences in color and texture.

Anna is originally from Sweden, but has since moved to Ottawa, Canada. As a child she was enamored with mythology and in university she took classes in Icelandic Sagas.

Anna holds a B.S. in Computer Science from Cornell University and an M.B.A. from Queens University.

www.knitandknag.com

THANKS

Special thanks to Hasmi Ferguson of Rocky Mountain Dyeworks who got so excited about the ancient Egyptian colors that she created a whole set of new colorways for this book, and most graciously supplied yarn in each of the six colors.

Thank you also to Sarah (Cephalopod Yarns), Claudia (Claudia Hand Painted Yarns), Kim (indigodragonfly), Gryphon (the Verdant Gryphon), and Roxanne (Zen Yarn Garden) for yarn and beautiful colors used in the book.

Many thanks to Alison Holley of Vancouver for her valiant test- and sample-knitting efforts.

And last, but not least, thank you to all the knitters worldwide who have knit my patterns over the years. Without you, this book would never have happened.

ABOUT COOPERATIVE PRESS

Cooperative Press (formerly anezka media) was founded in 2007 by Shannon Okey, a voracious reader as well as writer and editor, who had been doing freelance acquisitions work, introducing authors with projects she believed in to editors at various publishers.

Although working with traditional publishers can be very rewarding, there are some books that fly under their radar. They're too avant–garde, or the marketing department doesn't know how to sell them, or they don't think they'll sell 50,000 copies in a year.

5,000 or 50,000. Does the book matter to that 5,000? Then it should be published.

In 2009, Cooperative Press changed its named to reflect the relation-ships we have developed with authors working on books. We work together to put out the best quality books we can and share in the proceeds accordingly.

Thank you for supporting independent publishers and authors.

Join our mailing list for information on upcoming books!

www.cooperativepress.com

CPSIA information can be obtained at www.ICGtesting.com
Printed in the USA
LVOW010439220912

299876LV00001B/3/P